Edward N. Calisch

A Child's Bible..

Part I and II

Edward N. Calisch

A Child's Bible..
Part I and II

ISBN/EAN: 9783337171728

Printed in Europe, USA, Canada, Australia, Japan

Cover: Foto ©Lupo / pixelio.de

More available books at **www.hansebooks.com**

A CHILD'S BIBLE,

Being the Incidents and Narratives of Sacred Scriptures, Simply Told.

PART I.—FROM THE CREATION TO THE DEATH OF JOSEPH
PART II.—FROM THE BIRTH OF MOSES TO THE ENTRANCE OF THE PEOPLE INTO CANAAN

PARTS

EDWARD
(Rabbi of CONG. BETH

RICH
EZEKIEL &

Copyrighted, August 1894, by EDWARD N. CALISCH, in the office of the Librarian of Congress, at Washington, D. C.

A CHILD'S BIBLE.

CHAPTER I.

I.—THE CREATION.

Now, my young readers, I want you to think backwards as far as you can. Think back, oh, ever so long ago; think back of the time before you were born, before the city in which you live was built, long before this country was found out by Columbus, long before Columbus lived; think back as far as you can. Long before this time you are thinking of there was a time when there was nothing at all; no countries, no trees, no streams, no fish, no birds, no animals, no sun, no moon, no stars, nothing, except God. Then God made this earth as it is; not in one day, but in six days. At first the earth was without any shape or form, and everything was dark. Then on the first day God said: "Let there be light;" and the light came. On the second day He separated the earth from the heaven, and made the earth for itself with the splendid blue sky of heaven above it; and so came heaven and earth. On the third day He separated the water and the land. The dry land He called the earth, and the water He called the sea. Then He made all the beautiful things that are on the earth, the fine trees that give such nice shade and fruits, the pretty flowers with their sweet smell, and all the grains and vegetables that give us bread and food. On the fourth day He made the big, bright, glorious sun that shines on and gives us light by day, and the pale, silver moon, with the thousands of laughing, twinkling stars, to keep the night from being altogether black. On the fifth day He filled the air with the birds and their pleasant songs; all kinds of birds, and also on the same day all the fish in the sea. On the sixth day came the cattle and all kinds of animals; and last of all—man. On the seventh day God stopped His work and rested, showing us that we, too, must rest on the seventh day, and do no work at all. ——o——

II. ADAM AND EVE.

The first man was called Adam, and he was made in the *likeness of God. But when God saw that Adam was alone, all by himself, He said: "It is not good for man to be alone." So He put Adam into a deep sleep, and took one of his ribs and made a woman, whose name was Eve. Adam and Eve were the first people; and God put them into a beautiful garden, called The Garden of Eden. In the garden were all the good things that you

---

*When we say man is created in the likeness or image of God, it is not meant in body or figure, for God has no form or figure. He is a spirit of love, mercy, justice and truth. And man is made in the likeness of God, because he too is partly spirit, and can be loving, just, merciful and truthful. We must cultivate these virtues, because then we become more and more God-like.

can think of—the sweetest fruits, the nicest birds, and the finest trees and streams. And Adam and Eve could take whatever they wanted from anything, from any tree, except one, from which God told them they should not eat anything.

Now, the snake was the most sly of all the animals, and he coaxed Eve to eat. One day Eve was standing near the tree and the snake was there, and he asked Eve to eat some of the fruit of the tree. Eve told him that God told her "not to eat of the tree nor to touch it." The snake pushed her against the tree and said: "You have touched it, you might just as well eat of it." Then Eve ate some and gave some to Adam to eat, so they did not obey God.

And that is just the way it is with us now. It is the first step that is wrong. If your mamma tells you not to go out on the street and play, you will say: "Well, I will only go as far as the gate." And when you get to the gate, the boy on the other side will coax you out, and you will disobey you mamma just as Adam and Eve did God.

God was angry that they had done what He told them not to do, and drove them out of the beautiful garden, and told them they must now work for their bread. The snake was also punished. ——o——

III. CAIN AND ABEL.

Adam and Eve had two sons, named Cain and Abel. Cain was older than Abel, but he was wilder than his brother. He became a farmer. Abel was a shepherd, and loved to take care of the sheep and the lambs.

One day Cain and Abel brought each a present to offer up to God, to show their thanks for God's goodness. Abel brought his "offering," for so the Bible calls the present, from the best among his flocks, while Cain brought his from the fruits of the ground. God liked the offering of Abel, and took it, while He did not like Cain's. It was not because Abel's was better than Cain's, for everything belongs to God, and He gives us everything we have, and *what* we bring makes no difference to Him. But the reason was the *feeling* with which it was brought. Abel brought his with all his heart, but Cain was very unwilling, and would not have brought any if he had not seen Abel doing it.

Cain was now angry because God took Abel's offering, and not his, and he was full of envy against Abel. And he went away and sat down to think over it, and the more he thought the more angry he was with his brother, instead of putting the blame where it really was, with himself. While he was in such a humor Abel happened to come where he was, and Cain, full of envy, rose up and killed his brother.

When Cain saw his brother dead, and then thought what a terrible thing he had done, he ran away and tried to hide. But God called him and said: "Cain, where is thy brother Abel?" And Cain tried to deceive God and he said: "Am I my brother's keeper?" meaning to say: "How do I know where my brother is?"

Poor Cain, how unwise he was, trying to hide from God, who sees and knows everything. And some of us to-day try to do the same thing when we do wrong, though we do not do such a terrible thing as to kill anybody. Yet when you do wrong you try to hide it from your papa or mamma; but you cannot hide it from God, who will find you out even in the darkest coal-box in the cellar, or in the oldest trunk in the garret. He knows your sin just as he knew Cain's sin. He punished Cain, drove him from home, from his father and mother, and made him wander a long, long time, troubled by dreams of his murdered brother, till at last he stopped in a place called Nod.

God then gave another son to Eve, and she called him Seth.

IV. NOAH.

A long time after Cain had sinned and had been punished, about 1,600 years after God had made the world, there were very many people on the earth. But they were all wicked and bad, and did everything that was wrong, except one man, named Noah. Noah was a good and righteous man, and walked in the path that was pleasing to God. On account of the wickedness of the people, God said He would punish them and destroy them all by drowning, for He was going to bring a great flood over all the earth. But Noah and his three sons, Ham, Shem and Japhet, He saved, because Noah was a righteous man, and loved and obeyed God. But God, being, as He is, so good and kind, told Noah to build a ship, called an ark, and tell the people for what the ark was being built, and that if they would be sorry for their sins and would do better, God would not destroy them. But the people only laughed at Noah, and kept on sinning, and Noah kept on building the ark.

When the ark was finished God told Noah and his three sons, Ham, Shem and Japhet, and their wives and children, to go into the ark and close up everything. Noah also took in the ark with him all kinds of animals and birds, two of every kind that lived.

After Noah and his family, and all the animals and birds were in the ark, God "opened the windows of heaven," and caused it to rain, and the rain poured down for forty days and forty nights. And the water began to rise in the rivers over their banks, and the people went on the hills; the water came upon the hills, and the people went on the mountains; the water came slowly but yet surely to the mountains, and the people climbed up the trees on the mountain-tops; the water came up in the trees also, and the people could go no other place, and the water covered everything, and the people were all drowned.

But Noah, the God-fearing man, and his family, were in the ark, which rested safely on the surface of the water. For one hundred and fifty days was this so, and for one hundred and fifty days there was nothing to be seen but sky and water, and the ark on the water. At the end of that time the water began to go down. First Noah sent forth a raven from the ark; then he sent out a dove; but the dove flew to and fro and could not find a resting-place, so it came back. After seven days he sent the dove out again, and the dove came back with an olive leaf in its bill, and Noah knew that the earth was again beginning to be seen. He waited seven more days, and then went out of the ark with his family. The ark had rested on the top of a mountain, called Ararat. As soon as Noah came out of the ark he built an altar to God and thanked Him for having saved his life. And God was pleased that Noah was thankful, and He promised him He would not destroy the people by water again. Just then the beautiful rainbow came out and God said: "Let this be a sign of my promise. As long as you see this rainbow you will know that I will not bring a flood on the land again."

Now, when it rains, and you, my little readers, see the sun shine after the rain, and the rainbow with its many beautiful colors is seen, you will know that God has kept His promise, and you may be sure He always will.

But a long time after Noah, when the people were many again in the land, they forgot God and His promise, and tried to build a tower that would reach to heaven, and on which they could go if another flood came. And God, in order to punish them, mixed up all their languages. So they could not understand each other, and had to stop building, and all separate and go to different countries. The tower was called Babel, which means "confusion," because God confused all their languages.

CHAPTER II.

V. ABRAM.

If you have carefully read the last chapter you will remember that we learned about Noah and the flood, and the ark on Mount Ararat, and of the tower of Babel. Long after that time, about 400 years after Noah, there lived a man named Terah. Terah had three sons, Abram, Nahor and Haran. Haran died and left a son called Lot, and Abram took Lot into his own house and cared for him. In those times people did not worship God as they should, but had ugly figures of stone and blocks of wood to which they bowed down, and which they served. Terah, the father of Abram, also worshipped these idols, these images of wood and stone, but Abram did not. Terah even went so far as to make and sell these idols, and had a shop full of all kinds of figures. But Abram feared and loved the one true God in heaven, and so tried to teach the people around him. But he and his father could not agree, because Terah was an idolator, that is, he worshipped these stone and wooden idols. One day Abram heard the voice of God telling him to leave his father's house and go to the land of Canaan. So Abram took Lot, his nephew, and Sarai, his wife, and went to Canaan. Abram and Lot were both rich, had many cattle and sheep; for cattle and sheep were all the riches they had then, they had no gold and silver money and paper money like we have. Abram and Lot had so many cattle and sheep that they had no room for pasture, and one day there was a quarrel between the herdsmen of Abram and the herdsmen of Lot. Abram loved peace, and not wishing the quarrel to go on, he went to Lot and said: "We must separate; you may have your choice. If you wish to go to the right, I will go to the left, or if you choose to go to the left I will go to the right." Lot looked around, and saw that the plain of the Jordan was good land, and he went there and settled in the city of Sodom; and Abram stayed in Canaan. It was very good of Abram thus to separate without a quarrel, and we would get along a great deal better if we would act as Abram did. Some time after this, Lot was taken captive by some kings who were making war, and carried away, he, and all his property. When Abram heard this he took three hundred and eighteen of his men, and went and brought Lot back again. On his way back, the King of Sodom went to meet him and thanked him for bringing back his men. He also offered to reward Abram for his goodness, but Abram said: "No, not as much as a shoelace will I take; only what belongs to me and my men."

———o———

VI. THE DESTRUCTION OF SODOM.

Abram at this time had one son, whose name was Ishmael, and whose mother was Hagar. Sarai, Abram's wife, had no son, and God appeared unto Abram, and promised him that he would become the father of a great race, and that by him the earth would be blessed. God also changed his name, saying: "Thy name shall no longer be Abram, but Abraham, and thy wife's name shall no longer be Sarai, but Sarah.

Not long after this Abraham was sitting at the door of his tent, and he saw three men coming. Being a very kind man, he rose and ran to meet them, and asked them to come into his house and take some food and drink. They did so, and Abraham went to prepare the food. When he came back, one of them spoke to him and said that when he came back again, God would give Sarah a son whose name should be Isaac. They then rose and went away, and two of the messengers, for they were really messengers of God, went on to Sodom to warn Lot, that the city was going to be destroyed because the people in it were so very wicked. When Abraham heard that Sodom was to be destroyed, he prayed to God that if there were fifty good, righteous people in the city, God should not destroy it. But there were not fifty good people. Then Abraham prayed for forty, thirty, ten, righteous people, and God promised to save the city for the sake of the ten righteous people that should be found in it. But alas! there were not even ten good persons, and God was going to destroy the city, and another wicked city near it called Gomorrah. But Lot was a good man, so God, who never punishes unjustly, sent his messengers to save Lot. They came to the city, and Lot, who met them, asked them to come into his house, and they went in. But the wicked and bad people of the city came to Lot's house to ask who the strangers were. They came around the house and began calling out, and Lot went to the door and asked them not to act so wickedly. And then the men of the city pressed up around Lot even near unto the door; and the messengers took Lot in the house. The men of the city then rushed to the door, and God struck all of them with blindness for their wickedness. Then the messengers told Lot to pack up his goods and flee from the city, for God was going to destroy the city with fire and brimstone, and they told him not to look back at the city to see it being burnt. Then early in the morning Lot fled to the mountains with his people, but his wife did not obey God's message and looked back, and was turned into a pillar of salt.

———o———

VII. ISHMAEL AND HAGAR.

Abraham was still living in Canaan with his wife, Sarah, and with Ishmael and Isaac. Ishmael was a very wild boy and was always outside and seldom at home. Sarah was afraid that if the two boys kept together, Isaac would also become wild by being so much with Ishmael. So she told Abraham to send Ishmael and his mother, Hagar, away from the house. Abraham did not want to do so at first, but not wishing to have a quarrel in the house, and God also having told him to do as Sarah said, he called Hagar and Ishmael to him. He gave them some food and drink and told them to go away. And Hagar took the food and the skin bottles of water (for they had no glass then) and went into the desert. She wandered in the desert and her stock of water gave out, and Ishmael became sick, even unto dying. Hagar could not see her boy die, her mother's heart could not stand it, and she put the child under the shadow of a bush, and turned aside to pray to God. Think of that scene, my dear readers; the hot sands of the desert, the burning eastern sun, the dying child under the bush, and the sorrowing mother on her knees before her God. And Hagar prayed to God with all her soul; and, it seemed in direct answer to her prayer, she heard a sound as of falling water, and she turned and looked, and lo! she saw a tiny stream of water trickling from a rock. Joyfully she sprang to it, filled her bottle with its clear water and saved her child. Ishmael got better, grew up to be a man, a mighty hunter, and the father of a great race.

―――o―――

VIII. THE BINDING OF ISAAC.

Isaac meanwhile grew up to be a fine and splendid boy, and Abraham loved him with all his father's heart. One day, when Isaac was about thirteen years old, God appeared to Abraham and spoke to him as follows: "Take thy son whom thou lovest, thy son Isaac, and offer him up as a burnt-offering." When Abraham heard this command of God he was very, very sad. Isaac was his only child, and he loved him so dearly, and thus to lose him was too much. But his love for God was even greater, so with a heavy heart he went to obey God's bidding. He took the wood and bound it upon a beast of burden, took two servants and went to the mountain. When he came near the mountain, he told his servants to wait for him, and he and Isaac would go alone. As they two were going along, Isaac said, "Father, I see the knife for the offering and the wood for the offering, but where is the lamb you are going to offer?" Ah, little did Isaac know he was to be the lamb, or how his simple words must have cut the heart of his father. But Abraham only answered, "God will provide a lamb for Himself," and they went on. They went up the mountain and Abraham built the altar, arranged the wood upon it, and bound Isaac and placed him upon the wood. Then he raised the knife to strike it into the heart of his boy, when he heard a voice calling, "Abraham, Abraham." And he answered, "Here I am." And the voice said, "Lay not thy hand upon the boy, nor harm him." And Abraham looked around and he saw a ram caught in the bushes by its horns, and he took the ram and offered it up instead of his son. Then God said, "Now I know thou lovest and fearest Me, because thou didst not keep back from Me thy son, thine only son. And I will bless thee and thy possessions, and I will make thy descendants like the stars in heaven and sand upon the seashore for number." And Abraham and Isaac went back in joy and peace to their home.

———o———

IX. DEATH OF SARAH—MARRIAGE OF ISAAC.

Sarah was now getting old, and she died at the age of 127 years. Abraham went to the land of Hittites, and as a burial-ground bought the Cave of Machpelah. Ephron, the man who owned that piece of land, wanted to give it to him, but Abraham would not take it as a present, but paid the price for it, as he wanted to be entirely independent. He buried Sarah in the Cave of Machpelah.

Abraham, too, was now getting old, and he wanted to see Isaac married and settled down. As he was afraid Isaac might marry one of the daughters of the worshippers of idols, of the people around him, he took his servant Eliezer and made him promise he would get a maiden of his own people for his son Isaac. Eliezer promised, and he took some camels and he went to the city of Nahor. When he came near the city he saw the young girls drawing water from the well. And he asked God to help him choose a good wife for his master Isaac, and he took a sign that when he would go up and ask for a drink of water for himself, and the girl would of her own accord offer to give his camels water, he would know she was the right one. For he knew that if a girl had the kind heart to take care of the poor dumb animals, she would be a good wife. When he came near the well, he asked one of the maidens for drink, and she gave him a drink and asked, "Shall I give your camels water also?" And Eliezer was glad, for he knew she was the one to be Isaac's wife. He asked her name, and she said she was Rebekah, the daughter of Bethuel, the son of Nahor, the brother of Abraham. And Eliezer went with her to her father's house, and the next morning she went back with him and became the wife of Isaac. Some years after this Abraham died, when he was 175 years old, and he was buried in the Cave of Machpelah, beside Sarah, his wife.

——o——

CHAPTER III.

X. ESAU AND JACOB.

You remember, my children, how Eliezer got a wife for Isaac, how he found her out by her kind heart, by her caring for the poor, tired camels, then how Rebekah (often spelled Rebecca), went home with Eliezer and became the wife of Isaac. Esau and Jacob were the names of the two boys who were children of Isaac and Rebekah. Esau was a little older than Jacob, but there was just the same difference in their habits as there was in the characters of Cain and Abel, but Esau did not do such a terrible thing as Cain did. You remember Cain, how wild he was, always outside, always hunting, always in the woods, never at home; just so was Esau, and he went out in the woods so much that he became almost like a wild man, and had hair on his body just like the wild beasts that he hunted. But just as Abel staid at home and cared for the flocks and sheep, so did Jacob. But Isaac loved Esau the better, and Esau was his favorite, while Jacob was the favorite of Rebekah. Esau, being the elder, had the birthright, you know what that is, don't you? Well, it means that, being the eldest born, he had the right to his father's property when his father died. You know that it is so nowadays, for instance, when a king dies, his eldest son goes to the throne after him; that is his birthright. And Esau had this birthright, but he did not keep it the way he ought to. The birthright does not only mean the right to the property; it has other meanings, the oldest son, getting the largest share of the property, must also get the largest share of troubles. He must be the helper and guide of his younger brothers and sisters; he should look after them and care for them, be kind to them, love and protect them in all cases; he should so act toward them that they look to him as a second father, for, indeed, if it has pleased God to call the father away, to whom does the sorrowing wife and mother look for aid? up to whom do the fatherless children look, but to the oldest son, the one who has the birthright? All this is meant by the birthright, and all you who may be the possessors of the birthright and may read my words, are you sure you keep your trust the way it should be kept? Esau did not, and he therefore did not deserve to have it, and he lost it. One day Esau came home from hunting and was very tired and hungry. Jacob was near the house eating some pottage. Esau said, "Give me some pottage, for I am hungry." Jacob answered, "Sell me your birthright and I will give it to you." And Esau said, "Of what use is my birthright to me?" and he sold it for the pottage. So Esau despised the birthright, and therefore lost it.

——o——

XI. THE BLESSING.

Isaac, being a good man and worshipping God, led a peaceful and happy life, and God blessed him with plenty and with much riches. But he was growing old, and indeed, was almost blind, being so old. So, wishing to give his son his last blessing, before he died, (for a father's dying blessing is a sacred, precious thing), he called his favorite and eldest-born Esau to him. He told him to prepare for him a nice dish of venison (deer meat) and then he would bless him, and Esau went out to get it. Rebekah overheard this, and she wanted Jacob to get the blessing. She called him to her and told him to kill a sheep and she would prepare it for him, and he should take it unto his father and get the blessing.

Jacob did as Rebekah told him, and then put a skin over his shoulders, with the hairy side out, and went into Isaac. When he came in Isaac was somewhat surprised that he had come so quickly, and he said: "Who art thou?" and Jacob answered: "I am Esau, thy first-born." Isaac felt him then, and said: "The voice is the voice of Jacob, but the hands are the hands of Esau." Then he took the meat and blessed his son, saying that God would give to him of the dews of heaven, and that nations would serve him, and he closed with the words: "Cursed be any one that curseth thee, and blessed be those that bless thee." Jacob then went out. After a little while Esau came in to get his father's last blessing, and Isaac then knew how Jacob had deceived him, and Esau was very angry and said in his heart he would slay his brother.

Rebekah knew that Esau, when he found out

what Jacob had done, would want to hurt him and told Jacob to leave his father's house and go away for fear of his brother. Oh, what fearful results of deceiving! Here was the poor, old, blind father filled with grief because of the action of his son, the mother, compelled to send her best-beloved away from home, anxious because of his danger in wandering alone in the wilderness, the one brother full of anger and vowing to slay his brother, and the other brother fleeing away, away from father, mother, home, from all, out, out in the wilderness, fearing and fleeing for his life, and all this caused by deception.

———o———

XII. JACOB'S DREAM AND HIS MARRIAGE.

Jacob journeyed on, on, all day till night came on and found him out in the field, all alone, no house, no tent, no man, no being in sight. He took a stone for his pillow and lay down in the open field to rest. As he lay there, no roof above his head, except God's blue sky, he saw the sun sink in the west and go down out of sight, he saw the stars come out, one by one, and the weary wanderer's thoughts turned toward his God. Jacob was sorry for the wrong he had committed, and resolved hereafter not to trust to himself but to put his faith in God. Thus thinking of his Creator, he sank peacefully to sleep beneath the open sky, dotted with the millions of twinkling, laughing, stars. In his sleep he had a dream, a vision. He saw the sky part and he looked into the realms of heaven, and there he saw, in his dream, the eternal God seated on His throne of glory, and a ladder stretched from heaven down to earth, and countless angels were going up and down on the ladder—and God spoke to him and said: "Behold, I am with thee, fear not, where thou goest I will keep thee." And Jacob awoke out of his dream, and took the stone which had been his pillow, and set it up as an altar to God, and went on his way glad and happy.

Soon he came to a place where there was a well, and there was a large stone over the well. And Rachel, the daughter of Laban, who was the brother of Rebekah, came near to water the flocks of her father. Then Jacob rolled away the stone of the well for her, and told her he was Jacob, her cousin, the son of Rebekah, who was the sister of Laban. And Jacob went to the house of Laban, and became Laban's shepherd, and served him for some time. Then Laban said: "It is not right thou shouldst work for me for naught, tell me what thy wages shall be." Jacob said, "I will work seven years if thou wilt give me thy daughter Rachel as a wife." Laban promised. After seven years, when Jacob came to claim Rachel, Laban gave him Leah instead. Jacob said, "What is this thou hast done? Thou didst promise me Rachel and thou dost give me Leah." Then Laban said, "It is the custom in this country that the elder daughter be married first. Therefore I gave you Leah first. You work seven more years and you shall have Rachel." And Jacob did so, and Rachel also became his wife. Jacob had now served fourteen years when Laban told him that from now on all the spotted and speckled sheep and cattle should be his wages. And Jacob agreed and worked six more years for Laban and all the speckled cattle and sheep were his wages.

---o---

XIII. JACOB'S RETURN.

After he had thus been with Laban twenty years, the desire came to him to see his father and mother and his brother, Esau. He saw also, because God had greatly increased his cattle, that Laban was no longer friendly to him. So one day, when Laban had gone away to shear the sheep, Jacob took his wives and children and put them on camels, and took all his speckled cattle and went away. When Laban came back and heard that Jacob was gone, he immediately went after him and pursued him for seven days, when he came upon him. But God in a vision told him not to harm Jacob, so when he came to Jacob he said: "Why did you go away without letting me say good-bye?" Then he and Jacob made a covenant, an agreement to be friends, and he went back home, while Jacob continued on toward his father's house.

Soon he came, and he thought bitterly of the time when twenty years ago he had left that home an outcast and a wanderer, with a brother's vow against his life. He knew not if Esau was still angry, but he took his best cattle and sheep and sent them as a present to Esau, telling the messengers that they should tell Esau that he was coming on behind. Soon the messengers came back saying that Esau was coming with four hundred men. And Jacob was afraid, and divided his men so as to protect himself and children as well as possible. But Esau was no longer angry, and he and Jacob met each other as brothers should, and kissed and wept with one another. Esau then returned to his house and Jacob went to a place called Succoth and remained there. Soon after this Isaac died, full of years and happy to see his sons together again.

Jacob lived in Succoth and then went to the land of Canaan, to which, you remember, Abraham had gone, and which God promised him should belong to him and his descendants. He had twelve sons and one daughter, whose name was Dinah. His sons' names are Reuben, Simeon, Levi, Judah, Isachar, Zebulun, Dan, Naphtali, Gad, Asher, Joseph and Benjamin. Reuben was the eldest and Benjamin the youngest. But Jacob loved Joseph more than all the rest, and next to Joseph he loved Benjamin, because they two were the only sons of Rachel, whom he loved, and whom he had first sought for a wife. And in his love for Joseph he made him a coat of many different colors.

CHAPTER IV.

XIV. JOSEPH'S DREAMS.

In our last chapter we learned about the love that Jacob bore for Joseph; also, that to show his love, he made him a coat of many colors. But, alas! Joseph's life, because of that coat, was not as brilliant as were its many hues. When Joseph's brothers saw that he was more beloved by their father than they all were, they became very jealous and envious. They hated Joseph because his father loved him. And what added to their jealously and increased their envy were two dreams that Joseph had, and which he was foolish enough to tell and boast about. The first dream he had was as follows: he dreamed that he and his brothers were binding sheaves* in the field, and that his sheaf arose and stood up straight, and the sheaves of his brothers bowed down and humbled themselves before his sheaf. When Joseph told his dream to his brothers they were very angry. They said to him: "Art thou indeed going to have power us, and rule us?" And they hated him the more for his dreams and his words.

But Joseph would not take warning that they hated him for his dream, and said: "Behold, I have dreamed another dream. I dreamed that the sun, the moon, and eleven stars bowed

---

*Sheaves are the bundles into which the wheat is bound when it is cut.

down to me." His father even now scolded him, saying: "Shall I and thy mother come and bow down to thee to the earth?" And his brothers envied him more and more.

———o———

XV. THE SELLING OF JOSEPH.

One day, not long after the occurrence of these dreams, the brothers of Joseph were feeding the flocks at a place somewhat distant from the house of Jacob. Jacob sent Joseph to call his brothers home. And Joseph went toward Schechem, and there a man told him his brothers were in the valley of Dothan. His brothers saw him coming at a distance, and as soon as they saw him their anger against him began to rise. They said to each other: "Lo! the dreamer cometh." And the more they spoke the more envious and the angrier they became, till some one said they should slay him and cast him into a pit; and their envy and anger had gone so far that they all agreed to slay their brother!—and only because he was more beloved than they; Oh, my young readers, beware of envy. It carries you beyond your power, and causes you to do things of which you will forever after repent.

But Reüben, the oldest of the sons of Jacob, was more reasonable than his brothers, and he said: "No, shed no blood; cast him into the pit, but shed no blood." (You see, Reüben wanted to come afterward and save Joseph, after the brothers had gone away.) So they took from him his coat of many colors, and cast him into the pit, "and the pit was empty, there was no water in it." Scarcely had they done this, when they looked and saw some merchants—some Ishmaelitish merchants, who, with their camels, were going down to Egypt. Then Judah said: "What good is it to us to slay our brother? Rather let us sell him to these merchants." And forthwith they sold poor Joseph to the Ishmaelitish merchants, who carried him away.

Some time after Reuben came to the pit to take Joseph out, and he was not there, and he rent his clothes and wept, and went to his brothers, saying: "The child is not there." The brothers said nothing, but took the coat of many colors, dipped it in the blood of a slaughtered lamb, and brought it back to Jacob. When Jacob saw the bloody coat he wept and said: "Alas! some wild beast has torn my son, my Joseph." And he wept and tore his garments. His children tried to comfort him, but he would not be comforted, for he said: "I will go down into the grave, mourning for my son." Thus poor old Jacob wept and mourned for the son, who had been taken from him because of envy.

———o———

XVI. JOSEPH IN EGYPT.

But let us follow Joseph. The Ishmaelitish merchants carried him to Egypt, and there he was sold again to a man named Potiphar, who was captain of the king's body-guard. And Joseph put his trust in God, and he found grace in the eyes of Potiphar, and Potiphar placed him in charge of all his house. But Potiphar's wife was a wicked woman, and wanted Joseph to commit some wrong act, which Joseph refused to do. This made her very angry, and when Potiphar came home she told him that Joseph *had* done that very thing which he refused to do. Potiphar thereupon took Joseph and cast him into prison.

Poor Joseph! he was punished for what he did not do, yet his faith and trust in God did not stop. He kept his belief in God, and did his duty as it was to be done. On account of his good conduct he was raised to be overseer over the rest of the prisoners.

He had thus been in prison for some time when two men, the chief baker and the chief butler of the king, were put in prison. One day Joseph noticed that these two men looked very sad, and being very kind-hearted, he asked them what it was that troubled them. They told him they each had had a dream, but did not not know the meaning of the dream. Joseph asked them to tell him their dreams, and, with the help of God, he would try to give the meaning of their dreams.

The chief butler told his dream, and said: "I dreamed and I saw before me a vine, on which there were three branches, with three clusters of grapes. And in my dream I saw that Pharaoh's* cup was in my hand, and I took the grapes and

---

*Every king of Egypt was called Pharoah in olden times.

pressed them into the cup for wine, and gave it to the king, and lo! he drank the wine I offered him." Then Joseph said: "The three branches and the three clusters mean three days; that the king took the wine that you gave him shows that in three days he will take you from prison and place you in your office again." Then Joseph turned to the baker and said: "What is your dream?"

The chief baker answered and said: "I dreamed, and in my dream I saw myself. And I had three white baskets on my head, and in the baskets were all kinds of meats and food for Pharaoh; but as I was going along, the birds came down and picked the food from out of the baskets on my head." Then Joseph told him and said: "The three baskets also mean three days, but that the birds picked the food shows that in three days Pharaoh shall take you out of prison and hang you, and the birds shall pick your flesh as they picked the food." Then Joseph turned to the butler and said: "When you get back again to your office, pray remember me and help me, for I have been stolen from the Hebrews, and am in prison here most unjustly." And the butler promised.

In three days it came to pass just as Joseph had said; the baker was taken out and hanged, the birds picked his flesh; the butler was taken and given his former position, but he entirely forgot his promise to Joseph, and Joseph was left in prison.

XVII. PHARAOH'S DREAMS.

About two years after the event with the butler and baker, the king had two dreams. He came to the palace and wished some one to tell him the meaning of the dreams. Then all the wise men and the magicians, the astrologers, and the diviners, all came to the king to tell the king his dreams and the interpretation thereof. But they all failed; none of them could do as Pharaoh wished them to, and Pharaoh wearied of all the trials. At last he said that whoever should make the trial and succeed, he would reward with splendid gifts; but no one knew how to interpret the dreams. Finally the butler thought of Joseph, and how he had told him of his dream, and the butler told the king of Joseph. Then Pharaoh said: "Let him be taken out of prison and brought here to tell me my dreams." Joseph was brought before the king, and Pharaoh asked him if he could tell the meaning of his dreams. Joseph said: "God will give Pharaoh a peaceful answer." Then Pharaoh said: "I dreamed I stood upon the bank of a river and looked about me. I saw beautiful, large fields, fruitful and productive. And while I looked, behold, seven good, sleek, fat kine came up out of the river and commenced to feed upon the meadows roundabout. Then there came seven lean, hungry kine up out of the river; and lo, they went and ate the seven fat kine, and yet themselves seemed to get no fatter.

Again said Pharaoh, "I dreamed again. In my

dream I saw some stalks of corn. On one stalk there were seven fine, fat, full ears of corn that were waving in the wind. On another stalk were seven hungry, thin, parched ears of corn; and the seven thin, parched ears consumed the seven good, full ears, and seemed not to be any better or fuller."

Then said Joseph to Pharaoh: "In your dreams the seven fat kine and seven full ears, that came first, mean seven years of plenty and abundance that are to come—seven years in which the earth will bring forth its produce, the herbs will sprout and the trees bend with the weight of their fruit, and man and animal shall have plenty and sufficient. But then the seven lean kine, the seven thin, parched ears, show seven years of famine that are to come after and devour the seven years of plenty. The earth will be barren, the herb will be withered, and the fruit on the tree will be lacking. But," added Joseph, "if thou art wise thou wilt provide and prepare for the years of famine. Do thou build storehouses and granaries, which thou wilt fill during the years of plenty, that Egypt will not lack in the years of famine, and all nations will come to buy corn from Egypt, and Egypt and thou will become great, and rich, and mighty."

"Thou hast spoken well," answered Pharaoh, "and I appoint thee as officer to oversee the building of these storehouses and the filling of them. Thou wilt be high in power; I and the throne only will be above thee."

So Joseph from the prison became a prince and ruler of Egypt. And as he had said, it came to pass. The seven years of plenty came and passed away, and Joseph built storehouses and filled them. The seven years of famine came and all countries suffered, while Egypt had plenty; and all countries came to Egypt to buy corn of Joseph. Among others, there came Joseph's brothers from Canaan, for in Canaan, too, there was famine. The brothers came to Joseph, and bowed down to him, and begged him to sell them corn. So Joseph's dream came true; he was a prince, and his brothers, who had treated him so badly, were bowing before him, though as yet *they* knew it not.

―――o―――

CHAPTER V.

XVIII. JOSEPH AND HIS BROTHERS.

In our last chapter we saw Joseph standing in all his power and might, as first ruler in Egypt, while his brothers humbly knelt before him. He knew them full well, but they did not know him. And Joseph did not make himself known to them, but spoke to them and said, "Who are ye?" They answered, "We are men come from Canaan to buy corn." Joseph said, "No, ye are spies, come to spy out the land." They replied, "No, we are honest men, of one family, come to buy corn." Then Joseph asked, "Have you a father, and is he alive and well, and have ye more brothers?" They answered and told him their father was alive and well, and they had yet a younger brother, Benjamin. Then Joseph said, "Being as you say, you are not spies, and have yet a brother, I will keep one of you as a pledge till you come again and bring your younger brother with you." And they were frightened and spoke to themselves and said, "What is this evil that has befallen us?" Then they begged Joseph that he should not ask this from them, they had lost one brother, and their poor father had grieved so, and now to rob him of his best-beloved would surely be too much. But no, Joseph was firm. "Ye cannot come again unless ye bring your younger brother." They went away mourning and grieving, and Joseph kept Simeon as a pledge till they came back. When they returned to their father's house, they told Jacob what the man had said, and they found every one his money in his sack, together with the corn, for so Joseph had commanded. This also was a bad sign to Jacob, for he thought evil things were again coming to him, and he said, "You have bereaved me of my children, Joseph is gone, Simeon is gone, and Benjamin ye shall not take with you."

―――o―――

XIX. JOSEPH AND HIS BROTHERS.
(Continued.)

"And the famine was sore in the land," and Jacob could no longer withhold. He said, "Go again and buy corn." Judah said, "But the man did tell us saying that we should not come if we did not bring our youngest brother with us, and if you send Benjamin with us we can go, but if not we can not go." But Jacob objected, his heart was already torn by the loss of two of his sons, and he was afraid of losing a third, his best beloved, his Benjamin. Then Judah stepped forward and said, "Trust the lad with me, I will be surety for him, from my hand thou shalt require him." Jacob yielded, but told them to take presents along for the man, and a double share of money, for their money had been left in their sacks last time; and Jacob thought it might have been a mistake. The brothers then went again to Egypt and stood a second time in the presence of Joseph, their brother, but unknown to them. His first question was concerning his father, Jacob, if he was alive and well. Then he lifted up his eyes and saw Benjamin, he asked, "Is this your younger brother that ye have brought with you?" They answered it was. Joseph could hardly keep back his feelings at the sight of his brother, but he told them to prepare, as he wanted to give them a feast.

When they came in he seated them according to their age, but kept Benjamin near him, very much to their surprise; and to Benjamin he gave the choicest and the best of the food and drink; and they all ate and drank and were merry with him. Joseph then commanded his overseer to "Go, fill the sack of each one with corn, and put every man's money back into the sack. But my silver cup put into the sack of the youngest." And the superintendent did as Joseph commanded. The next morning Joseph's brothers departed with their beasts of burden laden with the corn; and they were very happy that they were going home safely and Benjamin was with them and Simeon also, for he had been set free. They were not gone very long before Joseph sent the overseer after them, telling him to say to them that his master's cup, the silver cup, had been stolen by one of them. The overseer went after them and overtook them and said, "Ye are nice men, indeed. Ye repay good with evil. Ye have eaten and have drank with my master, and now one of ye has stolen his silver cup." They answered, "God forbid that any of us should do such a wicked thing. We will undo the sacks, and with whomever the cup be found, let him die, and we will be bondsmen unto thy master." They took down the sacks and lo, in each man's sack was found his money, but nowhere was the cup to be found till they came to Benjamin's, and in his sack was the silver cup. Then they tore their clothes and loaded again their beasts of burden, and Judah and his brothers came back once more into Joseph's presence.

——o——

XX. JOSEPH MAKES HIMSELF KNOWN.

When they stood before Joseph, he said, "What is this ye have done?" And Judah answered, "What can we say unto my lord, how can we speak, we are guilty, both we and the one who has taken the cup, and we are all servants unto my lord." But Joseph said, "No, the man in whose sack the cup was found, he shall be my servant. As for ye, ye may go in peace unto your father."

Then Judah stepped forward and spoke, "Pardon, my lord, let not thine anger be against thy servant, but permit me to speak unto thee. When my lord asked his servants, saying, 'Have ye a father or a brother?' we did answer we had an aged father and a younger brother. Then my lord said, "Bring your younger brother with you, ye can not come again except ye bring your brother.' We went back unto our father and told him the words of my lord. When our food was gone, our father said, 'Go up and buy a little food,' and we answered, we can not go except we bring our younger brother. And our father answered, 'My wife, Rachel, gave me two sons, one ye have taken from me, and now, if ye take this one from me also, and evil happens to him, ye will bring down my gray hairs in sorrow to the grave.' And when I came to thy servant, my father, and said, we cannot go back except we bring our younger brother with us, for so the man has ordered, I saw that the life of our father was bound up in that of our younger brother and I said, let the lad go along, I will be surety for him that no mischief shall befall him, and from my hands thou shalt require him; and he suffered the lad to go along, I being surety for him. Now, I pray thee, my lord, let me, thy servant, stay as bondsman in in place of the lad, for how can I go up unto my father and the lad be not with me? I would have to see the evil that would come to pass unto my father."

When Judah finished speaking, Joseph could no longer restrain his feelings. He sent all the other men from the room, and turning to his brothers, he said, "I am Joseph, thy brother, and is my father still alive?" His brothers could not answer, they were so terrified at his presence. Joseph said, "Come near unto me, I pray, I am your brother, Joseph, whom ye sold into Egypt. Be not grieved or angry with yourselves that ye sold me hither, for to preserve life, did God send me— for there has been two years' famine in the land, and it will be five years before there will be plowing and harvesting. So God, not you, has sent me here to save your lives." He fell upon Benjamin's neck and embraced and kissed him, and he embraced and kissed all his brothers. He gave all of them presents, sent presents to his father, and sent them home to bring his father up to him. When they went away Joseph said to them, "Do not fall out by the wayside," meaning they should not quarrel as they went home. It may seem to you that this is a very queer good-bye to say to them. But Joseph knew them well. He knew that as they went home they would very naturally talk about him, and his sale into Egypt. They would each one try to deny his share of it and blame it on another. So, blaming each other and denying their own share of the guilt, they would very soon come to quarrels. So, he simply said to them, "Do not fall out by the wayside." So I, though by no means a Joseph, say to you, even to-day, "Do not fall out by the wayside." If you have ever done wrong in company with others, do not afterward try to put the blame on others and away from yourself. It will be of no use and only lead to quarrels and further mischief. In such cases let by-gones be by-gones, they cannot be undone, let them alone, do not fall out with your companions on the wayside of life.

―――o―――

XXI. THE DEATH OF JACOB.

When the brothers came home and told Jacob that his son, Joseph, was still alive and ruler over Egypt, he would hardly believe them. But when they told him what Joseph had said, when he saw the wagons and presents which Joseph had sent him, his heart within him rejoiced, his spirit revived, he said, "Enough, Joseph, my son, is still alive, I will go and see him before I die." Then he, his sons, all their wives and children, and all his household packed together their goods and went to Egypt, and all in all, the number that went down to Egypt was seventy. On his journey he stopped at Beer-Sheba, and offered sacrifices to God, and God appeared to him in a vision of the night and told him that He would be with him to go down to Egypt and that he would see his son, Joseph. He went to Goshen, and Joseph came in his chariot to meet his father at Goshen, (Goshen was the richest part of the land of Egypt, and Pharaoh had given it to Joseph, for his father and brothers to live there). Jacob and his sons lived there and tended their flocks and sheep. Joseph brought his father and brothers before Pharaoh, and Jacob blessed Pharaoh.

After Jacob had lived in the land of Goshen for seventeen years he began to grow weak and he knew his time to die had come. All this time Joseph had been ruler in Egypt and ruled the land exceedingly well. Jacob called all his sons to him, and he blessed Joseph and his two sons, Ephraim and Menasseh, and he blessed all his other sons.*

When Jacob died his sons mourned for him thirty days. When the days of mourning were passed Joseph commanded the physicians to embalm the body. Then Joseph and his brothers took the body of Jacob and buried it in the Cave of Machpelah, where were buried Abraham and Isaac and their wives, Sarah and Rebekah. Jacob's first wife, Leah, was also buried there.

After his father's burial Joseph returned to Egypt and ruled the land long and well. When

---

*The dying blessing of Jacob is considered one of the most beautiful passages in the Bible. You will find it in chapter xlix., First book of Moses, Genesis. You will find it well worth your reading.

he was one hundred and ten years old his summons came to die, and his body was embalmed and put in a coffin in Egypt, and there was great mourning throughout the land of Egypt.

CHAPTER VI.

XXII. BIRTH AND EDUCATION OF MOSES.

At the time of the death of Joseph the Israelites were fully settled in the land of Goshen, and they increased wonderfully and grew mighty in number. Then the Pharaoh of Joseph's time also died, but the memory of Joseph and of his service to Egypt was kept alive in the heart of the king and his people for a long time. At length, as the Bible expresses it, "there arose a king who knew not Joseph," that is to say, he no longer remembered the good that Joseph had done for his ancestors and his country. The Israelites too had increased so much that the King Pharaoh began to fear them, and so he made them all captives and slaves, and they had to work for him, build all his buildings, do all his work and toil for him for nothing, for no pay at all. Their overseers and taskmasters were cruel and harsh and treated them very meanly. But in spite of all the harshness and cruelty and mean treatment, the Israelites thrived and grew mightier and mightier in number.

Heretofore they were supplied by the king with straw and stubble, with which they were to make so many bricks per day. If they did not furnish the required number of bricks they were whipped and beaten unmercifully. But as they increased, despite persecution and cruelty, the king one day sent forth an order, that henceforth no more material was to be supplied to the Israelites; they would be compelled to furnish their own straw and stubble, and still they had to *turn out the same number of bricks as before!* The people groaned aloud under this new affliction, but they groaned in vain. Their taskmasters only answered with the lash and the whip. But still they flourished and thrived; God blessed them, and their number rose higher and higher. Finally, the king, Pharaoh, gave forth an order that all the male children that would be born to the Israelites should be taken and thrown into the river Nile. This cruel command went forth, and great grief arose among the people. But their prayers and tears were of no avail; the heartless overseers and taskmasters went through the houses, and all the male children were cast into the Nile river. The poor helpless infants suffered for a single man's fear.

Among others there was a woman, named Jochabed; her husband's name was Amram, and to her was born a son. The boy was a beautiful lad, and the mother could not bear to give him up to the cruel overseers, to be thrown into the river, so she hid him and kept him from the taskmasters. This continued for about three months, when the lad grew to be big and strong, and she could hide him no longer. She took a basket and daubed it with pitch on the inside and outside so as to make it water-tight, lined and padded it nicely, and put the little child in the basket. She then took the basket and went to the bank of the river. There, offering up a short prayer to God, she put the infant in His charge, and pushed the basket with its precious freight out into the river. She watched it as it floated down the stream until it passed out of sight, then turned, and with a heavy heart went homeward.

The basket was not altogether unwatched, for the little boy's older sister followed it at the river's edge, to see what would become of it. It floated gently along, the child sleeping quietly and peacefully, as though in his cradle at home. At last, after going some distance, it stopped, caught in some bulrushes that grew in the water. The shock awoke the child, who, enjoying his new situation, laughed and crowed with delight. Very soon, the daughter of the king came down from the palace to bathe. As she came near to the water she heard the child, and looking around, discovered it in its little basket. "It is one of the Hebrew children," she said, and her heart warmed toward the child. She sent one of her maids to bring the child to the shore. Just then, the older sister, who had been watching all this time, with an anxious, beating heart, stepped forward and asked the princess if she wanted one of the Hebrew women to nurse the child. The princess said yes, and the girl hurried off to get the child's own mother. The child was taken to the palace, and brought up as though he was the son of the king's daughter, and was treated like a prince as long as he remained in the palace. That child was Moses,* our people's great leader and law-giver. His older sister was Miriam.

———o———
PART XXIII.

Moses remained in the king's palace till he was quite a man. He was taught and educated in all the knowledge and wisdom of the time. All that was fit for a prince to know or to have, he knew and had. But he could not speak well, that is, he could not speak plainly; he was no orator. There is a beautiful fable in the Talmud connected with this lack of oratory in Moses. The Talmud says that when Moses was taken by Pharaoh's daughter and brought into the palace all the wise men and magicians and astrologers, etc., said to the king, that if that child was allowed to remain in the palace he would do some harm to the king when he got older. Of course the king's daughter protested against this, saying, "What harm can come from the child?"

Finally after much talk a trial was agreed upon. The child was brought into the room and there

---

*Moses (Hebrew *Moshe*) is from the word *Mosha*, to draw. He was called so because he was drawn out of the river by Pharaoh's daughter.

were placed before him a beautiful ruby and a flaming coal. A child's first impulse is to put everything in its mouth. If it chose the ruby, that would show that it was an extraordinary child and knew what it was about and ought to be sent away, for it would surely work harm to the king.

When Moses was brought in, and the two articles were placed before him, he being an extraordinary child *did* take the ruby and was going to put it in his mouth, when the angel Gabriel, who was standing at his side, quickly changed it and gave him the flaming coal instead, which he put into his mouth, and burned his mouth, thus causing a defect in his speaking.

But Moses grew up to be a fine, strong young man, and being a true man, he was very much troubled about the persecutions and oppressions of his brethren.

One day as he was walking along he saw an Egyptian and an Israelite fighting together, and he stepped up to separate them, when the Egyptian turned upon him, and Moses slew him.

Soon after, when he went out a second time, he saw two Israelites fighting together. He tried to separate them, when one of them turned to him and said: "Who are you that do thus? Who made you a judge or an officer over us? Do you intend to slay me as you did the Egyptian?"

When Moses heard this he became afraid, for he feared that Pharaoh might find out that he had slain the Egyptian. So he fled from Egypt and went to the land of Midian. He sat down to rest by a well, and the daughters of the priest of Midian came to water their flocks. But the shepherds chased them away and would not let them come near the well. Then Moses arose and drove away the shepherds, drew water and watered the flocks of the maidens.

When they came home they told their father an Egyptian had helped them to water their flocks.

Then he said: "Where is the man? Wherefore have ye left him? Go call him that he may eat bread."

They called Moses and he came and was content to remain with the man, who gave him his daughter Zipporah as a wife. And Moses had a son whom he named Gershom, which means, "a stranger." "For," said Moses, "I was a stranger in a strange land."

———o———

PART XXIV.

Moses was the shepherd of Jethro, his father-in-law, and every day he took the flocks out to pasture, for them to graze and feed, and when evening came on he led them back to the fold again. One day in his wanderings with his flock to find pasture land he came to Mt. Horeb, the mountain of God. As he stood there by the mountain, he saw a thorn-bush which had caught on fire and was burning. As he stood and watched the burning bush he noticed that though the bush had been burning for some time it did not seem to be burnt up at all, but burned on and on and did not give out. Moses said to himself, "I must turn aside and see this wonderful sight, why the thornbush is not burnt."

And as he turned aside to see the wonders of the ever-burning bush, a voice, the voice of God, called to him from the midst of the bush, "Moses," and Moses answered, "Here am I." Then the voice called again and said, "Come not near unto this place: put off thy shoes from off thy feet, for the ground on which thou standest is holy ground." Moses took off his shoes and knelt down in sacred fear upon the spot, for the voice of God was speaking to him. The voice then continued and said, "I am the Lord, God of thy fathers, the God of Abraham, of Isaac and of Jacob. I have seen the affliction and distress of my people in Egypt and have heard the cry that has gone up from them because of their taskmasters: yea, indeed I know their sorrows, and I am come down to deliver them out of the power of the Egyptians and take them to a land that is good and rich and fertile, to a land flowing with milk and honey. Now then go. I send thee to Pharaoh, and thou shalt bring forth my people, the children of Israel, out of Egypt." Then Moses answered, "Who am I that I should go to Pharaoh, that I should bring the children of Israel out of Egypt?" God answered, "Do thou go, and I will be with thee, and this shall be the sign that I have sent thee, when thou hast brought out the people, thou shalt worship God upon this mountain."

Then Moses said again unto God, "But the people will not believe me when I come to them and tell them that I am sent by your God to deliver you out of Egypt. They will say, 'What is his name?' and then what shall I say unto them?"

"Tell them," answered God, "that the great, eternal and everlasting God, the God of their fathers, the God of Abraham, Isaac and Jacob, the almighty 'I am that I am,' has sent thee to them. Go, collect together the elders and chief men of Israel, and tell them that their God has come to take them out of Egypt to a land rich and fertile. Then they will hearken to thy voice, and then thou and the elders of Israel shall go unto Pharaoh and ask for the release of My people. But Pharaoh will not let thee go, and I will stretch forth my hand over Egypt and shall work wonders and miracles never seen before. Then my people shall go out, and each woman shall ask of her neighbor vessels, vessels of gold and vessels of silver and garments, and they shall put them on their sons and daughters, and they shall empty out Egypt."

But said Moses again: "They will not hearken unto my voice or believe me, they will say the Lord hath not appeared unto thee." Then God said, "What is that thou hast in thy hand?" Moses answered, "A staff." And the Lord said, "Cast it upon the ground." And he cast it upon the ground, and it became a snake. Moses became frightened and fled from it. God said, "Seize it by the tail." He took hold of it by the tail and it became a staff again in his hands. God said, "This will be a sign unto them that the Lord hath sent thee to deliver them." And furthermore said the Lord, "Put thy hand into thy bosom." Moses put his hand into his bosom and it became leprous, white as snow. God said, "Put thy hand again into thy bosom;" and when he drew it out it was again as his other flesh.. "Now," said God, "they will hearken unto thy voice and will believe thee, and if they do not, thou shalt take some water out of the river and pour it upon the dry land, and it will come to pass that the water out of the river will become as blood upon the dry land."

"Yet," said Moses a third time, "I can not speak to them, as thou knowest thy servant, I am heavy of speech and heavy of tongue." God answered, "Go to Aaron, the Levite, thy brother, he is a good speaker and he will speak for thee, and I will teach you both what you shall do."

Then Moses turned and went back to Jethro, his father-in-law.

———o———

PART XXV.

When Moses retured to his father-in-law, Jethro, he asked him if he could go back to Egypt to see how his friends were getting along, if they were alive and well, and Jethro told him to "go in peace." Then Moses took his wife and his son, and started for Egypt. On the way he met his brother Aaron, and he told him what they were to do together, and they both went on to Egypt. When they came to Egypt they collected together all the chief men and elders of the Israelites, and Aaron spoke to them the words which God had spoken to Moses at Mt. Horeb, and Moses did the wonders which God had showed him. The people then believed and trusted in Moses, and knew that God had seen their trouble and had heard their cry of sorrow, and had now come to help and to save them.

After that Moses went to King Pharaoh, and said to him that the Everlasting God of Israel demands the release of His people Israel, that they may go and hold a feast in the desert. But Pharaoh answered, "Who is this God, this everlasting One, that I should let the people go to serve Him? I do not know Him. I will not let the people go." Then when Moses and Aaron asked him again, he said, "Wherefore do you trouble the people and hinder them from their work? Go about your business, and let the people be." On that same day Pharaoh commanded his taskmasters and overseers not to furnish stubble or straw to the people with which to make bricks. They must gather their own straw, and yet each one must hand in the same number of bricks each day. You see, Pharaoh had set the Israelites to work making bricks, to build cities, and he furnished them with straw to make the bricks, and each was to hand in a certain number of bricks as a day's work. Now he commanded that they would have to supply their own material themselves and yet make the same number of bricks that they had made before. The poor Israelites suffered terribly under this new affliction and cried aloud in their distress, but it was of no use; the cruel taskmasters answered their cries with a blow of the lash and only increased their sorrow and pain.

When Moses came back the people spoke to him and said, "See what thou hast done. Thou didst promise to deliver us from the hands of the Egyptians and set us free, but thou hast only angered Pharaoh and made our work harder for us." Then Moses spoke to the Lord, and said, "Wherefore didst thou say I should go unto Egypt and free thy people? Is it for this thou didst send me! For since I have spoken to Pharaoh, he has hardened the work and the people do only suffer the more because of my speaking." Then answered God: "Now thou shalt see what I will do unto King Pharaoh, for with a strong hand will he send them away and drive them out of the land."

―――o―――

XXVI. THE TEN PLAGUES.

"Now," said God to Moses and Aaron, "go up unto Pharaoh and command him to let my people Israel go, or I shall smite him with sore and grievous plagues." Moses and Aaron went to Pharaoh, and Pharaoh asked a miracle from them to show that they had come in the name of God; Aaron took his staff which he had in his hand and threw it upon the ground, and it turned into a serpent. Then Pharaoh called all his wise men and magicians, and they too cast each one his staff upon the ground, and it turned into a serpent, but the staff of Aaron swallowed up the staffs of the wise men. But yet the heart of Pharaoh was hardened and he refused to let the people go. Then God commanded Moses, and he sent the first plague upon Egypt. He stretched forth his staff over the river of Egypt and all its water became blood; so also the water in all the wells and cisterns, in all the jars and vessels and crocks, all the water throughout the land of Egypt was turned into blood, and there was no water to drink. The Egyptians had to dig wells away from the river bank to get water to drink. But yet Pharaoh would not let the people go, for his magicians had also changed the water into blood. Then Moses brought the second plague upon Egypt. By the command of God he spoke to Aaron, and Aaron stretched his staff out over the waters of Egypt, and out of all the waters of Egypt there came up frogs. From every pond, river, creek, well and cistern, frogs came up and spead themselves over the entire land of Egypt. Every house was full of frogs, frogs were everywhere, and the whole land was horrible because of frogs.

Then Pharaoh became sick. He called unto

Moses and Aaron and told them: "Only take these frogs away from my land and I will let your people go to serve their God." Moses stretched his staff again over the land and all the frogs died out of the land. They gathered them together into great heaps and the whole land smelled horribly because of the frogs.

When, however, Pharaoh saw that the frogs were all gone and the land was free from them, he got over his fright and he refused then to let the people go. When Moses heard this, by the command of God, he stretched forth his hand over all the dust of Egypt, and all the dust of Egypt became vermin and insects upon every man and woman and child in Egypt, and also upon all the beasts, the cattle, the oxen and the sheep. But the land of Goshen, where the Israelites lived, had none of these plagues, not the blood nor the frogs nor the vermin. The magicians and the wise men of Pharaoh also tried to do the same, to bring the vermin, but they could not, and they cried out, "It is the finger of God." But Pharaoh's heart was hard and he hearken not to what they said. Then God said to Moses, "Go place thyself before Pharaoh, as he goeth down to the water, and tell him that the Lord God says, "Let my people go that they may serve me. If he will not let them go I will send against him and all his house wild beasts, and all the houses of the Egyptians shall be full of wild beasts. But I will make a distinction," said God, "that the land of Goshen, where my people are, there shall be no wild beasts, that Pharaoh may know I am the Lord God of Israel." But Pharaoh was stubborn and would not let the people go. So Moses sent the wild beasts, that went into every house in Egypt, and the whole land was laid waste because of the wild beasts. Then Pharaoh called to Moses and said, "Go, sacrifice to your God, go, but do not go very far from me, I pray you. Go, but take these wild beasts from me." Then Moses prayed unto God and God removed the wild beasts from the land.

But again when Pharaoh saw that there was a rest, that the wild beasts were removed, his heart again became hard; he became stubborn, and would not let the people go.

So Pharaoh did after each plague. God would send a fearful plague upon him, and while it was there he would promise to let the people go. But when the plague was gone he would break his promise and not let them go. So he did for ten plagues, four of which I have already mentioned to you, and of the rest I will tell only the names, for it all happened the same way. Pharaoh would yield while the plague was there, but became stubborn again after it was gone, until the last great plague, when he drove the Israelites out of the land. The first nine plagues are: (1) blood, (2) frogs, (3) vermin, (4) wild beasts, (5) murrain,* (6) boils, (7) hail, (8) locusts, (9) darkness. You

---

*Murrain is a sickness that affects oxen and cattle and sheep, etc.

must remember that from all these plagues the children of Israel in the land of Goshen were free, and so also in this great and fearful, last and tenth plague.

---o---

XXVII. THE LAST AND TENTH PLAGUE.

God thought that now with these nine plagues he had punished Pharaoh enough for all his cruelty to the people of Israel, so He determined He would send one more plague that would be so terrible and so fearful that Pharaoh would be glad to get rid of the Israelites. He commanded Moses to tell the Israelites that each one should take a lamb and slaughter it, offer it up to God, and sprinkle its blood upon the door-posts of the houses. For that night the Angel of Death was going to pass through the land at midnight, and he would visit with death every house upon which there was *not* sprinkled the blood of the lamb.

Moses commanded the Israelites, and each man slaughtered a lamb and sprinkled its blood upon the door-posts of the houses. Moses also told them to make themselves ready to go, and be prepared to leave at any time, for now the moment of their freedom out of Egypt was at hand.

Everything was in perfect readiness, and that night, at the hour of midnight, God's Angel of Death went through Egypt and knocked at the door of every house on which there was not the blood of the lamb. And in every house there died on that night the first-born child, the first-born of the king as well as the first-born of the lowest slave, and also the first-born of the cattle. But the houses on which the blood was sprinkled the angel passed over, and in them no one died.

Then Pharaoh and his people awoke, and there arose out of Egypt such a cry as had never been heard, or shall ever be heard, for there was not a house in which there was not one dead.

Then Pharaoh called unto Moses and Aaron in the night and said, "Rise up and go forth from among my people. Go, serve your God as you have spoken." Then Moses called to all the people and they rose up and went out of Egypt. They went in a great hurry and they took their bread with them unleavened. And each woman had asked her Egyptian neighbor for vessels of gold and silver, and for garments. These they took along with them, and they emptied out Egypt. Their bread which they had taken with them they baked into unleavened cakes, for they had no time to leaven it. And that is the reason when Pesach comes along that we to-day eat *Matzos*, for they are unleavened cakes, and they remind us of the time when our forefathers went out of Egypt from slavery to freedom. So also our Feast of Pesach reminds us of what the people suffered then in captivity, and we think how we are free and happy to-day. We think how God cared for his people and took them out of slavery, worked so many wonders for them, punished Pharaoh for his cruelty and wickedness to them. We think also how God has so kindly kept and guarded our forefathers from that time to the present day, how he has always been with them, has fought for them and helped them, till to-day we are a free and happy people in a free and beautiful land. Ought we not, dear children, be thankful and grateful to God for all His mercies and kindness?

CHAPTER VII.

PART XXVIII.

My dear children, you remember that in our history last time we came out of Egypt with the children of Israel. Pharaoh, the king of Egypt, had been smitten with ten fearful and dreadful plagues ending with that last, most terrible of all, the death of all the first-born children of Egypt. Then in the middle of the night of the fourteenth of Nissan,* the Israelites rose up and went out of Egypt. The number that went out of Egypt was 600,000 souls,

The Israelites went on their way glad and rejoicing, for they had left behind them a life of trouble, sorrow and slavery, and were now entering upon a new life of happiness and independence. Besides God was with them, for He went before them with a pillar of cloud by day and a pillar of fire by night, to show them the way and lead them. Moses also was with them, that same brave man

---

*Nissan is the first month of the Jewish calendar.

who had dared to stand before the king of Egypt and demand the release of the people of God. So with happy hearts they went out of their home of slavery, and they took with them the bones of Joseph, for when Joseph died he had made the Israelites promise that they would take his bones with them when God would take them out of Egypt.

Happily then they followed the pillow of cloud by day and the pillar of fire by night, and it led them, not through the land of the Philistines, for the Philistines were enemies and there might be war, and the Israelites were not prepared to fight, but by a roundabout way and they at last encamped at the edge of the wilderness, and near the Red Sea.

When Pharaoh heard that the Israelites were encamped between the wilderness and the sea, he said to himself: "They are caught in the land, and the wilderness has shut them in. I will go after them and catch them again." You see Pharaoh felt very sore that the Israelites had left him, for it was to him the loss of 600,000 persons, who had worked for him for nothing, for the Israelites had been his slaves. So he made ready all his army, took six hundred fine, chosen chariots, and all the rest of the chariots in Egypt and went after the Israelites to bring them back to Egypt. He came upon them as they were encamped by the sea.

When the Israelites saw Pharaoh with all his chariots and his immense army come up behind them, they were greatly frightened. There was the sea stretching out in front of them, the great forest and wilderness lying around them, and the dreaded Pharaoh, with his army, behind them. They had no way by which they could flee, and in their terror they cried out against Moses and said to him: "Is it because there are no graves in Egypt that you bring us out to die here in the wilderness? Is it for this you brought us out of Egypt? It is better for us that we serve the Egyptians than to die here in the wilderness." But Moses answered, "Wait and see the help which God has prepared for you. Do you keep quiet, God will fight for you."

———o———

XXIX. THE CROSSING OF THE RED SEA.

That night the Israelites slept peacefully in their camp, for the pillar of cloud, that had been in front of them, went behind the camp and stood between them and the army of Pharaoh, so that the two came not unto each other all the night. That night, too, God caused a wind to blow from the east and it drove back the sea and made it dry land. When the Israelites awoke in the morning, Moses led them and they followed him, on dry land through the sea, and the waters stood up as a living wall on the side of them. Pharaoh and his army too awoke, and great was their astonishment to see the Israelites slip from their hands and escape through the sea. Pharaoh immediately commanded his army to move forward and follow the Israelites into the sea. But the Israelites were already on the other side and safe out, and God caused the sea to go down and it swept over Pharaoh and his whole army and they all were drowned, horses and riders, king and soldiers, all were drowned in the mighty sea through which the Israelites passed safely under the guidance of God.

The Israelites were now happy and joyful, God had again helped them and they had seen with their own eyes how their enemy and persecutor, the cruel Pharaoh, with all his immense army, had been destroyed in the sea.

They sang and danced and were happy at their deliverance, but Moses called their attention and showed them how it was that God had helped them, and had destroyed their enemies. He told them that they should sing and give thanks to Him, and Moses himself composed a beautiful song in praise of God (which, if you want to read, you can find in the fifteenth chapter of Exodus, the second Book of Moses). And Miriam, the sister of Moses, the one who had watched him as he floated down the river Nile, also sang a beautiful song in honor of God. And now the people feared God, and believed in Moses, His servant.

In this happy frame of mind, Moses led the children of Israel away from the sea to the wilderness of Shur. Here they journeyed for three days, but could find no water to drink. Their supply of water had given out, and the people were beginning to get anxious on account of the lack of water, when they came to Marah where there was water. They all joyfully and eagerly went forward to drink the waters of Marah, when lo! the waters were bitter, they could not drink them. At this disappointment, together with the want of water, the people forgot all about God and His goodness, forgot all the good that Moses had done to them, and murmured and rebelled against Moses, saying: "What shall we drink?" Moses prayed unto God, and God showed him a tree which he cast into the water, and the water became sweet. And the people drank and were satisfied.

XXX. THE MANNA.

From the waters of Marah in the desert of Shur, Moses led the Israelites first to Elim, where they encamped a short while. From Elim they went to the desert of Sin. It was now the fifteenth day of the second month after their departure out of Egypt. Being most of the time in the desert where they could get no food of any kind, the food which they had brought with them out of Egypt was almost gone, and in many cases entirely gone.

They became frightened, and in their fear and fright they forgot that God was watching them, they forgot that the Almighty Being who had taken them out of Egypt, had punished Pharaoh with ten fearful plagues, had led them with a pillar of cloud by day and a pillar of fire by night, had carried them safely through the Red Sea, and had drowned therein Pharaoh and his great army, had sweetened for them the bitter waters of Marah, they forgot that this same almighty and good God was still watching over them, and they cried out against Him and Moses saying: "Would that we had died by the hand of God in Egypt, where we sat by our flesh-pots, and had bread to eat to the full. Why hast thou brought us out here in the wilderness to kill us all with hunger?"

Alas, how forgetful the people are of all the goodness of God. They go along day after day, and are loaded with blessings and good things, but never stop to think who gave them to them, or to thank Him. But the moment a bit of trouble comes upon them they turn to God they had neglected in their prosperity and cry to Him for help. Ah, my dear children, think how many good things you have, and stop a moment to thank the Giver of all good, for He is watching you to-day, as he did the Israelites in the Wilderness of Sin so many thousand years ago.

Moses at this new rebellion of the people turned to God, and God said to him: "I will let rain bread from heaven, and the people shall go out and gather it, only a certain portion every day. And it shall come to pass that on the sixth day they shall gather a double share of what they gather every day." Moses then turned to the people and said: "At evening ye shall know that it is God who has led you out of Egypt, and in the morning ye shall behold the glory of God which He will prepare for you."

In the morning when the people awoke, there was around the camp a layer of dew, and when the layer of dew was gone, there was upon the face of the wilderness something very fine in grains, very much like hoar-frost. And when the children of Israel saw it, they said unto one another, it is "Manna," for they knew not what it was. And God commanded that each man should gather every day an "omer"* full for every person in the house. Each man should gather according to his household. On the sixth day they gathered a double share, for on the morrow, on Sabbath, the day of rest, no manna fell, for it was a holy day, a day sacred to God.

———o———

XXXI. THE FIGHT WITH AMALEK.

From the Desert of Sin the Israelites continued their journeyings, and after some time they encamped at Rephidim. Again here at Rephidim there was no water for the people to drink. You must remember, dear children, that in the desert there is nothing on which a person can live. There is no flower nor tree nor bush, nor vegetation of any kind; nor are there any streams or ponds or any kind of water. All is sand, sand, trackless sand, as far as the eye can reach. You look to the right and you see the sand stretching away, away

---
*An omer is a measure used among the Hebrews.

till you can see no more, and the heaven comes down and kisses the sand; you look to the left and you see the same, the sand reaching out until the sand meets the sky. And so is on any side you may look. It was only by the goodness and care of God, which gave them food and drink that the Israelites were able to journey in the desert. Now again they came to a place where they had no water to drink, and again they forgot all the good that God had done to them before, and cried out against Moses, saying: "Why did you bring us out of Egypt to kill us and our children and our cattle."

Moses, however, had firm faith and trust in God, and this faith and trust never misled him. He turned to God in this new trouble, and God said to him: "Take thy staff which thou hast in thy hand, and go before the people and smite upon the rock at Horeb; and there shall come forth from it water, and the people shall drink."

Moses did so before the eyes of the elders and people of Israel. He smote the rock, the water came forth and the people drank. And he called the place Massah and Meribbah, because of the quarreling and rebellion of the people.

There was an idol-worshiping nation near Rephidim, named Amalek. When Amalek heard that the people of Israel were encamped at Rephidim, that nation came up to fight with Israel. Moses, when he saw Amalek coming, told Joshua to choose for himself men to fight Amalek, and Moses,

Aaron and Chur went up on the mountain. Joshua did as he was told, chose the men, while Moses and his companions went up on the mountain. Joshua fought with Amalek, while Moses on the mountain held up his hand and prayed to God. As long as Moses held up his hand in prayer to God the Israelites conquered Amalek, but when Moses took his hands down Amalek got the better of Israel. So Aaron and Chur held up the hands of Moses, and when the sun went down Moses was holding his hands up in prayer to God, and Israel conquered Amalek, who fled from before Israel.

Now, my dear children, you must not think that the holding up of the hands of Moses was the cause of the defeat of Amalek, for surely that did not make Amalek weaker in men or Israel stronger in men. But it did make Israel stronger in spirit, for when they saw Moses holding up his hands in prayer to God, they knew that God was with them on their side. So they fought with greater courage and more spirit because of their faith in God, and their faith in God helped them win the battle from Amalek. So, also to-day, dear children, you should put you faith and trust in God, and it will give you better feeling, more courage, and greater spirit; and you will be the victor in the battle of life in which you are daily engaged.

―――o―――

XXXII. THE VISIT OF JETHRO.

After this battle, so grandly won, Moses led the Israelites a little farther in the desert and encamped them in the wilderness. While he was here Moses received a visit from Jethro, his father-in-law. Jethro was a Midianite, and Moses had married his daughter, Zipporah, at the time when he had fled from Egypt and had gone to Midian to seek refuge. Now Jethro came to him, bringing with him the wife and two sons of Moses. The names of the two sons were Gershom* and Eliezer.† Moses was greatly rejoiced to see his father-in-law and his wife and his children, and he went out to meet them. When Jethro and Moses had met and greeted each other, Moses told Jethro all that God had done for Israel, how He heard their cry in Egypt, when the cruel taskmasters imbittered their lives, how he had brought them out of Egypt, through the Red Sea, through the desert and through many other dangers, had carried them by the power of His great love and kindness to the place and the time where Jethro now saw them, contented and happy because of their recent victory over Amalek. When Jethro heard all this he rejoiced greatly and said, "Blessed be the God who has delivered the people out of the hand of Pharaoh and out of the power of the Egyptians." Jethro also built an altar and sacrificed before God with all the elders of Israel.

It happened one day during Jethro's visit to

---

*The word Gershom means a stranger there. Moses named him so because he was a stranger in the land of Midian, when the lad was born.

†Eliezer was so called because "God" was the "help" of Moses in rescuing the Israelites.

Moses that Jethro stood by while Moses judged the people; and the people stood around Moses from morning until evening. As Jethro remarked this he said to Moses, "What is this thou dost, that thou sittest alone and the people stand around thee from morning till evening?" Moses answered, "I sit here to judge the people, because the people come here to inquire of God. When they have a matter of dispute they come to me, and I judge between one man and his neighbor and make them know the laws of God." Then the father-in-law of Moses answered him: "But it is too much for thee, thou will surely wear thyself away, and also the people that is with thee, thou canst not do it alone. Now hearken to me and take my counsel," he continued, "thou shalt be the mediator between the people and God and shall let the people know the laws of God; but moreover thou shall select from among the people able men; men of God; men who love truth; men who care not for their own gain, and these thou shalt set to judge the people, so that it will be easier with thee. For the light and easy matters they shall judge and the weighty ones only shall come unto thee." Moses hearkened unto the voice of his father-in-law and did all that he had said. He chose good, honest men, who judged the people well, and only the difficult matters came to him. Then Jethro went back unto his land again.

——o——

CHAPTER VIII.

XXXIII. THE TEN COMMANDMENTS AT MT. SINAI.

After the departure of Jethro, Moses led the Israelites onward till, in the third month after their coming out of Egypt, they encamped in the wilderness of Sinai, opposite the foot of the mountain.

There God appeared to Moses and commanded him to tell the people they were to get ready and come to the foot of the mountain, as then the glory of God would appear from the mountain. Moses did as God had told him, he ordered the Israelites to prepare themselves to approach the mountain, but he set bounds that they should not come too near. On the third day the people assembled at the foot of the mountain, and the power and glory of God began to make itself manifest. There were thunders and lightnings rolling along and flashing forth from the heavens; a heavy cloud was upon the mountain, the sound of the cornet mingled with the roar of thunder, and before all this manifestation of God the people trembled and became afraid. Then Moses made an offering unto God, and sacrificed peace-offerings. For six days the glory of God was apparent upon the mountain and on the seventh day Moses went up the mountain. He was gone on the mountain forty days and forty nights, and while on the mountain he was with God, who gave him the following:

TEN COMMANDMENTS.
(Exodus xx, 2-14.)

I. I am the Eternal thy God, who brought thee out of the land of Egypt and out of the house of bondage.

II. Thou shalt have no other Gods before Me. Thou shalt not make unto thee any graven image, or the likeness of anything that is in the heavens above, or on the earth beneath, or in the waters under the earth. Thou shalt not bow down to them nor serve them, for I the Eternal thy God, am a jealous God, visiting the iniquities of the fathers upon the children to the third and fourth generation of them that hate Me, showing kindness unto the thousandth generation of those that love Me and keep My commandments.

III. Thou shalt not take the Name of the Eternal, thy God in vain, for God will not hold him guiltless, who taketh His Name in vain.

IV. Remember the Sabbath day to keep it holy. Six days shall thou labor and do all thy work, but the seventh day is a Sabbath to the Eternal thy God. On it thou shalt do no work, neither thou, nor thy son, nor thy daughter, nor thy manservant, nor thy maid-servant, nor thy cattle, nor the stranger that is within thy gates. For in six days God made heaven and earth, the sea and all that is therein, and ceased His labors on the seventh day. Therefore God blessed the Sabbath day and hallowed it.

V. Honor thy father and thy mother, that thy days may be prolonged in the land which the Eternal thy God giveth thee.

VI. Thou shalt not kill.

VII. Thou shalt not lead an impure life.

VIII. Thou shalt not steal.

IX. Thou shalt not bear false testimony against thy neighbor.

X. Thou shalt not covet thy neighbor's house. Thou shalt not covet thy neighbor's wife, nor his man-servant, nor his maid-servant, nor his cattle, nor anything that is thy neigabor's.

———o———

XXXIV. THE GOLDEN CALF.

When Moses had been gone on the mountain for some time the people began to get impatient at his long absence. They inquired about him of Aaron, but he could give no news of him. His absence continued, and their impatience changed into low muttered grumblings, and from indistinct grumblings it finally broke out into open remonstrance and rebellion. They came storming to Aaron and angrily demanded the whereabouts of Moses, saying: "Where is this man Moses? Up, make us gods that shall go before us, for we know not what has become of that man Moses who brought us out of Egypt." Poor Aaron, unused to leadership, unused to withstand the foolish anger of the people, did not know how to act, so he said to them, "Take out all the golden ear-rings which are in the ears of your wives and your sons and your daughters and bring them to me." He thought that the people would not be willing to give up their golden ornaments, and so he could escape complying with their angry demand for a god. But in this he was mistaken. The people brought to him their gold. He took it, made a mould and cast the gold into the shape of a calf. When Aaron saw the golden idol, he said, "These are thy gods, O Israel, that have brought thee out of Egypt." He then proclaimed that there would be a feast unto this god on the morrow.

The people rose up early the next day, came near unto the idol and offered it burnt-offerings and peace-offerings. They sat down to eat and drink and then arose and sang and danced around the golden calf, worshipping it with all the enthusiasm of their savage nature.

Meanwhile God spake to Moses on the mountain and said, "Go, get thee down, for the people which thou hast brought out of Egypt is wicked and corrupt." Moses, with the two tablets of stone in his hands, turned and went down the mountain, where he had been for forty days and nights for the sake of that ungrateful people, now dancing around the golden calf at the base of the mountain. When he came near he heard the voice of singing and as he drew near enough to see, his righteous anger and indignation knew no bounds. He seized the two tablets of stone, and with all his force dashed them to pieces at his feet. Then he stepped boldly into the midst of the sinning

Israelites, took their golden calf, ground it into fine powder, and cast into the water, so that the people could drink their god. Then he turned to Aaron and said, "What has this people done that you have brought upon it such a great sin?" Aaron explained that the people came to him clamoring for a god and he took their golden rings and cast it and the form of a calf came out.

Moses saw that the people had become unruly, so he placed himself at the gate of the camp and said, "All who are on the side of the Lord, let them come unto me." There came to him all the tribe of Levi.* He told them they should punish the idolators and many of those who had bowed down to the golden calf were killed.

God told Moses to hew two more tablets of stone like the first two and bring them to Him. Moses brought the two tablets and went again up on the mountain of Sinai, where he stood a second time in the presence of God.

―――o―――

XXXV. THE BUILDING OF A TABERNACLE.

Soon after this Moses gathered together all the people and spoke to them as follows: "Thus says the Lord your God: 'Let all those of willing heart

---

*From this time on, because of its righteous action, the tribe of Levi was consecrated to God and became the priests and teachers of the people. Formerly every first-born son of every family of each tribe was to be a priest, but from now on this holy duty was given to the Levites alone.

bring to me offerings for the building of the Tabernacle, offerings of gold and silver and copper, offerings of cloth and yarn, of blue and purple and scarlet yarn, offerings of wood and of skins, offerings of oil, oil for lighting and oil for anointment, and offerings of onyx stone and other precious stones, and also all the skilful and wise among you shall come to do all that the Lord has commanded." You will notice, my dear children, that the verse expressly says "those of willing heart." Such only were the offerings that God desired, not those that were brought with grumbling and reluctance, but only such as came with the heart of the giver; came with joy and gladness to do something to show gratitude to the great and good God that had given them so much and had done so much for them. So also to-day, my dear young readers, of all the good things and blessings that you enjoy, remember that they have all been given to you by God, and if He should ask anything from you, do you give it gladly and with a willing heart, and you will build up a tabernacle of peace in your own heart, as did those Israelites many years ago in the wild and sandy desert, built a tabernacle of glory and beauty to the God who had done so much for them.

When all had been collected together, Moses called for architects,* builders, masons and workmen, and with them built a temple, a tabernacle

---

*The architects who are specially mentioned in connection with the building of the tabernacle, are Bezalel and Aholiab, of the tribe of Dan.

according to the following plan: The length of the tabernacle was thirty cubits, and its height ten and its breadth ten. Each side of the tabernacle was made up of twenty boards of acacia (shittim) wood, each board plated with gold, and fastened to its neighbor by sockets of silver; each board ten cubits high and a cubit and a half wide.

For the rear or westward end of the tabernacle, there were six boards, with two end boards for the purpose of joining the end firmly to the sides.

At the opposite or eastern end, which was the entrance, there were five wooden pillars richly carved and ornamented with gold. Over these pillars there was a beautifully embroidered curtain of bright and rich colors, and this curtain formed the entrance of the tabernacle.

The ceiling was made of fine and strong linen, also embroidered in beautiful designs, rich in color. Spread over this was a covering made of goat's hair, upon this a covering of skins, and upon this still a fourth, made to keep the tabernacle safe and dry in all kinds of weather.

The tabernacle was divided into two divisions; that which divided them was another beautiful curtain, hung upon four wooden pillars, wrought with gold and beautiful designs. The larger apartment was toward the east, or entrance, of the tabernacle, and the western apartment, an exact cube of ten cubits high, ten long and ten broad, called the holy of holies.

XXXVI. THE FURNITURE OF THE TABERNACLE.

In the eastern part, called the sanctuary, or holy place, there were the "golden candlestick" and the "table of show-bread."

The candlestick was made of purest beaten gold, with a central shaft and three branches on either side rising to equal height with the central branch, forming thus seven sockets for seven lights. The central shaft, and branching arms as well, were made of exquisitely figured and purest gold Everything that belonged to the candlestick, its bowls and tongs and snuff dishes, all were of finest gold.

In the sanctuary there was also the table of show-bread. It was like a small, ordinary table, upon four legs. But it was overlaid with gold, and around its edge was a rim or crown, also of gold. It had two long poles attached to it running through golden rings and projecting out at either end. These poles were for the purpose of carrying the table. On it, arranged in two piles, were twelves loaves or cakes, according to the twelve tribes of Israel. They were replaced every Friday by fresh loaves, by the priests.

A third article in the Sanctuary was the altar for burning incense. It was made of acacia or shittim wood, was one cubit long, one cubit broad and two cubits high. It was plated with gold, and sweet incense was burnt thereon, in honor of the Lord, every morning and evening.

All the articles hitherto described were in the eastern and large apartment, called the Sanctuary, but in the western division of the tabernacle there was only one, called the "Ark of the Covenant." It was a box made of wood, plated with gold, but its lid, or cover, was not plated, but was of the purest of that precious metal. This also had a rim or crown around it. On the lid were placed two figures of gold, the figures of cherubim or angels, kneeling, facing each other. Their arms were folded over their breasts in form of prayer, and their outspread wings, of purest gold, projected over above their heads so far that they touched one another. The lid of the ark beneath the outspread wings of the cherubim was called the Mercy Seat, and within the ark were the two tables of stone inscribed with the Ten Commandments, which Moses had brought down from the mountains.

The Holy of Holies which contained the ark of the covenant, was kept always dark, and no one dared to enter it, not even Moses himself, no one could enter except the high priest, and he only once a year, on Yom Kippur, the Day of Atonement, when he went in to atone for the sins of the people.

This was the tabernacle proper, built under the direction of Moses from the offerings brought by the people, brought from their own willing hearts for the temple and glory of God.

——o——

XXXVII. THE OUTER COURT.

The tabernacle was surrounded by a much larger inclosure, called the court. This court was one hundred cubits long, and fifty broad. Around this was the fence, made of pillars, twenty on each side, and ten at each end. These pillars stood in sockets of brass and were held together by means of rods, from which curtains were suspended.

Within this space, called the court, stood the altar for burnt-offerings. It was made of brass-plated acacia wood. It was about five cubits long, five broad, and about three cubits high. It had a horn at each upper corner. On it were sacrificed the daily burnt-offerings of the people, and on it also was kept alive the continual sacred fire. The ash-pans into which the ashes of the offerings fell, as also the tongs, shovels, etc., were made of copper, kept brightly polished and burnished.

In the court there was also the brazen laver, for the priests. As its name signifies it was made of metal, and the metal was supposed to have been made of the metal mirrors of women who served at the tabernacle. It was a large basin resting on a pedestal, or base, and in it was kept water for the use of priests, who were require to cleanse themselves ere they entered upon any sacred duty.

Into the court all the people were allowed to enter, and it stood unroofed, the smoke from the burnt-offerings going unimpeded to the blue sky above.

The tabernacle stood at the western end of the court, its entrance facing the east and the rising sun. At the western end of the tabernacle stood the Holy of Holies.

And just think, dear children, the whole of this beautiful tabernacle, with all its golden plates, the silver sockets, the magnificently embroidered curtains, rich in color and in design, the golden candlestick, the table of show-bread, the ark of the covenant, with the cherubim bending in ever sacred silence over the golden mercy-seat and curtain—all this surrounded by the richly carved and curtained pillars of the tabernacle, and again surrounded by the beautiful flowing robes of the court, all this, think, dear children was made from offerings brought by willing hearts and the work done by the willing hands of the Israelites in the desert. And yet they did nothing but what they should have done, for all they had and all we have is from God, and there can be no more fitting use of it than to be again dedicated to His service.

---o---

XXXVIII. THE GARMENTS OF THE PRIESTS.

After the building of the tabernacle had been finished God called unto Moses and told him to take his brother Aaron and sanctify him as high-priest, and that the tribe of Levi should become the priests of the people.*

---

*This was because of the virtuous action, at the time of the worship of the golden calf.

The garments of the high-priest consisted of four different pieces, each piece woven of the finest and richest cloth and embroidered with most beautiful work. The largest garment, or the robe (in Hebrew the מְעִיל M'eel), reached from the shoulders almost to the ground. At the bottom it had a hem, to which were attached small golden bells. This robe was, however, shorter than the linen shirt or tunic worn under it, which extended to the ankles. Above the robe was worn the Ephod (אֵפוֹד). This was a still shorter garment, fastened at each shoulder by precious stones engraved with the names of the tribes, and caught at the waist by a belt, or girdle, made of the same finely-wrought work of which the Ephod was made.

Upon his breast the high-priest wore a breast-plate, called the breast-plate of judgment (חֹשֶׁן הַמִּשְׁפָּט). It was of the same material as the Ephod, and on it, in three rows, were twelve precious stones, again representing the twelve tribes. In the breast-plate was also the Urim and Thumim, which was consulted by the high-priest for the people in times of danger.

And lastly upon his head the high-priest wore a head-dress or turban, called a mitre (מִצְנֶפֶת). In the front was a small golden plate inscribed with the words, "Holy unto God." Such were the holy garments of the high priests; those of the common priests were simply white linen garments with a colored girdle.

CHAPTER IX.

XXXIX. THE SIN OF NADAB AND ABIHU.

One day, Moses, at the command of God, took Aaron and his sons and placed them before the assembled people. Then, in the presence of all the people, he put upon Aaron the robe and Ephod, and girded him with the belt of the Ephod. He also put upon him the breast-plate and the Urim and Thumim; and upon his head he placed the holy mitre with its golden plate toward the front. Then Moses poured the oil of anointment upon the sanctuary and all that was therein; he also anointed the beard of Aaron, then blessed Aaron and the sanctuary, declared the latter sacred unto God, and Aaron and his descendants ever after, devoted to His service, the anointed of the Lord.

They were to conduct the services of the sanctuary, they had the care of all the holy vessels, to keep them pure and clean, ever ready for service, and they offered up all the offerings of the people. All this they did in accordance with fixed rules and laws, laid down in the book of Leviticus, for the time of the service, the manner of the service, the garments of the priests, etc. And Aaron and the other priests did as Moses had commanded. But one day two sons of Aaron, named Nadab and Abihu, came before God with strange offerings and a strange manner of worship, and for their wickedness and presumption they were punished by God with death. God also commanded Aaron and the rest of his sons not to weep for the two who had been killed, for they had been wicked and sinful, and the punishment which they had received was just and righteous. This tells us, that to-day, when wrong is done and committed, we should not sympathize or weep with the sinner and wrong-doers, nor try to shield them from punishment, for punishment and sorrow is ever the result of sinfulness, and reward and gladness that of goodness and virtue.

---o---

XL. KIBROTH HATAAVAH.

The rest of the book of Leviticus is occupied with laws and statutes, governing the conduct and lives of the Israelites, the kinds of offerings they had to bring, the times when these offerings were to be brought, and the manner in which they were to be sacrificed. Not wishing to burden you with this, which can have no interest and application to-day, we will pass over to the next book of Moses, the fourth book, called Numbers. It is called Numbers because therein is found the numbering of the Children of Israel, that is, that Moses numbered them each according to his tribe; each tribe had a certain banner or standard, and each tribe occupied a certain position on the march. For now they had begun to march through the desert to the land of Canaan which God had promised to give them, a beautiful land, a "land flowing with milk and honey." On their march, too, they expected to be attacked by the different nations through which they passed, and so they were put not only in marching order, but also in fighting order.

But, notwithstanding all the good Moses did for them, and all the care he took of them, the people grumbled and were dissatisfied. We saw how they complained for food and God so miraculously supplied them with food by the manna. Now the foolish people had grown tired of the manna and cried out against Moses and against God, "they wanted meat to eat, they were tired of the manna, they remembered how they had had fish and meat to eat in Egypt, and now they wanted meat to eat." Poor Moses! at this new dissatisfaction of the people he knew not what to do. He turned to God and begged him to relieve him of the burdens of this people for they were too much to bear. But God answered, "I will supply them with meat." And Moses was astounded and said, "Will flocks and herds be killed for them that they may have meat, or will all the fish in the sea be gathered together that they may eat?" God answered, "Is My hand too short, or My power too little that I can do this? Go thou unto the people and tell them they will have meat." Moses did as God had told him, and the people were quiet. That night God caused a strong wind to blow, and in the morning the people found about the camp countless numbers of quails. They greedily began to eat them, and God's anger became aroused against them, he sent among them a plague. Many died because of their greediness and were buried there, so the place was called Kibroth Hataavah, "graves of lust," because the people had lustfully craved for meat, and many had come to their graves because of their lust.

———o———

XLI. AARON AND MIRIAM—THE SPIES.

Not only did Moses have to suffer from the rebellions of the people at large, but every single person went against him; his own sister and brother, Miriam and Aaron, and (as we will learn later on) a man named Korach.

Aaron and Miriam spoke against Moses because of his wife, that she was not an Israelitish woman. For, you remember, Moses had married Zipporah, the daughter of Jethro, the priest of Midian. They also said, "Is it only with Moses that the Lord has spoken, has He not also spoken with us?" God heard this, as He hears, sees and knows everything, and He commanded the three, Moses, Aaron and Miriam, to go unto the tabernacle. There appearing in a pillar of cloud, He said, "Now you will know that Moses is My true servant, that unto him I am seen face to face, while to other prophets I am seen only in a dream or in a vision." Then the cloud disappeared from the tabernacle, and when Aaron turned to Miriam, lo, she was leprous, white as snow. Aaron very humbly begged forgiveness of Moses and of God, and he and Moses prayed to God to heal Miriam. So He did, but Miriam had to stay outside of the camp for seven days, for she was unclean because of the leprosy.

After Miriam had become better, the people journeyed on until they came to the wilderness of Paran. They were now near the land of Canaan, near the good, rich land which God had promised to give to them. Moses gathered the people together, picked out twelve men, one from each tribe,* and sent them to spy out the land, to see if it was rich and fertile, and if the Israelites could go up and take possession of it. The spies went into the land and they came to the valley Eschol. There everything grew large, rich, and abundant. They cut down from a branch a cluster of grapes and it had to be carried by two men, and they carried back with them other fruits. At the end of forty days they finished spying out the land and returned to the people to give their report.

"Truly," said they, "it is a land flowing with milk and honey, as these fruits can testify, but (and here they added grievous falsehoods) the land is filled with giants, the children of Anak. They are so large that we look like grasshoppers by the side of them, and their cities are all large and strongly fortified. We are not able to go up against them, for they are stronger than we are." At this the people cried and wept aloud, "Why have you brought us here in the wilderness to die?

---

*The twelve tribes are: Reuben, Simeon, Judah, Issachar, Ephraim, Benjamin, Zebulun, Menassah, Dan, Asher, Naphtali and Gad.

Would it not have been better for us, our wives and our children to have died in Egypt than to come here and die by the sword in a strange country?" But two men, who had been with the spies, Caleb, the son of Yephunneh, of the tribe of Judah, and Joshua, the sun of Nun, of the tribe of Ephraim, they alone tried to quiet the people, telling them it was not so, that the people were no larger than ordinary and that they could go up and easily conquer the land. But the people would not listen to them and continued their cries. Then the anger of God was kindled, and He determined to punish the people one and all with fearful punishment. But Moses prayed to God in behalf of the people, saying that the nations of the earth would say that God had taken the Israelites out of Egypt, but was not able to bring them into the land of Canaan, as He had promised. Thereupon, God, for the sake of His faithful servant, Moses, punished the people with the punishment that none of those living now should live to enter the blessed land as He had promised; they would be compelled to wander forty years in the desert till all those present would die and their children would then take possession of the land; except Joshua, the son of Nun, and Caleb, the son of Yephunneh, they only, because they told the truth, they would enter the promised land. So the Israelites were compelled to wander forty years in the desert and in the wilderness, because of their rebellion and want of faith in the Almighty.

XLII. THE REBELLION OF KORACH.

When now the Israelites had begun their forty years' wanderings, they were very much displeased and grumbled a great deal. Especially one man of the tribe of Levi, named Korach, was loudest in his grumblings.

He and two men, Dathan and Abiram, of the tribe of Reuben, together with about two hundred and fifty men, whom they had gathered about them, came before Moses and said to him: "You assume too much, for the whole congregation is holy; the Lord is with them all, why do you place yourself above the rest?" Moses answered Korach, "Is it too little for you that God has separated you and the tribe of Levi, to be sacred and holy unto Him, to stand before the congregation? For this beware, both you and all your company, for ye have placed yourselves against God." Then he called for Dathan and Abiram, but they would not come up, and sent the answer back to Moses, "Is it too little that you have brought us out of a goodly land here to the wilderness for us to die, and you wish to make yourself prince over us? Moreover you have not brought us to the land of milk and honey which had been promised to us." At this Moses became very angry and said to Korach, Dathan and Abiram, "To-morrow do you and all your company appear before the Lord, each man with his censer."* The next day came and as the

---

* A censer was a small lamp used for burning incense. It was attached to chains and carried and swung by the priests.

assembled people were standing before the tabernacle, among them Korach and his company, a fire came down from heaven and consumed the company, while the earth opened and swallowed up Korach, Dathan, Abiram and the other leaders of the rebels. At this fearful sight of God's anger the people fled in terror, but as soon as they saw that all danger was over they murmured against Moses and Aaron, saying that they had caused the death of all these men. God then commanded Moses that he should take a staff from each tribe, the tribe of Levi included this time, thus making thirteen staves. Moses did so, and placed the thirteen staves at the door of the tabernacle. In the morning, when the people came to the tabernacle, they saw that the staff of Aaron, which represented the tribe of Levi, had budded, blossomed, and brought forth almonds, while the other staves had simply remained as they were. By this sign it was proven that Aaron was the true high priest.

——o——

XLIII. THE SMITING OF THE ROCK.

After peace had been restored the people continued to march on in the wilderness to spend the forty years which, in their blind folly, they had brought upon themselves. They had not proceeded far before their supply of water had given out; the water was gone from out their skin bottles, and so was the courage from their souls, and the satisfaction from their minds. They began to scold and grumble once more. They raised their old cry, "why had Moses brought them out here in the wilderness to die!" They remembered how they had had enough to eat and drink in Egypt, where the vine, the fig and pomegranate grew, but now Moses had brought them out in the desert, where nothing grew, there was no water, and they and their cattle must die.

Again Moses turned to God for help, and God told him to gather the people together at a certain rock, there to speak to that rock and the water would come forth plentifully for all the people.

Moses gathered the people as God had directed him, but instead of merely speaking to the rock, he smote it twice with his staff. The water gushed forth in an abundant stream. The people drank to their heart's content, and filled their bottles again with the precious fluid. I say precious, because the water is truly precious, though it may seem hard for you to think so, you who have water around you all the time and as much as you want. But if you should ever be in such a position (but I hope you never will be), where water is scarce and hard to get, then realize what a truly precious thing it is, how sweet that clear, pure fluid is, that God has so kindly given to us, and in such abundance.

Then again we can begin to realize the great mercy and goodness of God, when we think how mercifully He provided this life-giving fluid for those thousands of souls whom He in His infinite kindness had taken from their slavery in Egypt, to give them a beautiful and fertile land, a land flowing with milk and honey.

Here we have the first and only case where Moses, the kind, the patient Moses, did not follow out the exact letter of God's command. God had told him only to speak to the rock for the water to come forth, instead of that, Moses struck the rock twice with his staff. On account of this disobedience Moses was punished that he could not enter the holy land, but must die when the Israelites had finished their forty years' wanderings.

It may seem to be a great punishment for a light crime, but we must remember it was disobedience to God's law, and it was more the principle of *disobedience* than any gravity of crime. How careful we must be then not to disobey any law of God, and we must constantly be on the watch, for it is so easy to sin.

———o———

XLIV. THE SERPENT OF BRASS.

Not long after their trouble with the water the Israelites were again sorely troubled. They were attacked by serpents, for in their marching they came to a place where countless numbers of snakes were, and these went in among the people biting and poisoning many. The Israelites became greatly frightened when, they saw so many of their number sick and dying; they came to Moses begging him to help them. Moses caused a brass serpent to be made, and put it at the top of a high pole; all those that were bitten by the serpents were to pass under this brass figure of the serpent. They all did so.

Those that looked upward as they passed were cured and saved, but those that kept their eyes fixed down sullenly on the ground remained uncured, and died.

The reason of this was that those who looked upward, looked up to, and put their faith and trust in God; but those that kept their eyes fixed on the ground had lost all faith in Him and thus were punished by death, while the faithful and trusting ones were saved.

How readily we can see that that applies to us to-day where it is so easy to be bitten by the serpent of sin, which is ever low and earthly, and those that look upon it will suffer from it, while those that put all trust and faith in our Heavenly Father will escape from its snare. When you see temptation, look away from it, look up to God. Do not look down to it. You can not withstand it—get out of its way.

———o———

XLV. THE WARS.

Although all troubles and quarrels among themselves were quieted and peace dwelt in the camp of the Israelites, yet they had to be on their guard, for they had now entered upon the last stages of their desert exile, and were rapidly approaching the boundaries of Palestine. But between them and that wished-for land of promise, there were several idolatrous tribes, through whose land they must pass in order to reach their goal.

Foremost among these were the *Edomites*, the people who inhabited the country of Edom. This country lay directly south of Palestine, and just in the way of the Israelites, who came upon it first. When they had come to the boundaries of Edom, the people of Israel sent messengers into the land, begging permission to go through, and promising not to rob, injure or hurt anything belonging to the Edomites, but these messengers were harshly received and sent back with the answer that no permission would be given.

At this the Israelites were angered, but remembering that the Edomites were related to them (they were the descendants of Esau, the brother of Jacob), they determined not to return evil for evil, and so turned out of their path, going to Mount Hor.*

After journeying for some time they came upon the country of the Amorites, and Moses sent to Sihon, their king, the same request, namely, to be allowed to pass quietly through the land. Sihon refused, and not only refused, but also gathered together an immense army and came out to do battle against the people of Israel. But God was with the Israelites and they conquered Sihon, put him to death and took possession of his land.

---

*It was here that Aaron died, aged one hundred and twenty-three years. He was greatly mourned for by the Israelites, and Eleazar, his son, became high priest in his stead.

Next they came upon the land of Bashan, of which Og was king. When he heard that the Israelites were approaching his country, he too, gathered together a large army and went to fight against them. But he also was conquered and his land taken possession of. So, with God on their side, the Israelites marched victoriously on toward the good land which was to be to them an inheritance forever.

———o———

XLVI. BALAK AND BALAAM.

Leaving the land of Bashan they come next upon Moab. Balak, the King of Moab, heard of their approach, and knowing what they had done to the Amorites, and to the people of Bashan, he became greatly frightened.

There lived in those times a man named Balaam, the son of Beor, and he was a great sorcerer and diviner. It was said of him that he could fortell the future, that he had power over the lives of animals and man, that whatever he cursed became accursed, and upon whatsoever he bestowed a blessing, upon that object came blessing, but with all his power he was nevertheless in the power of God, as we shall see.

When Balak, the King of the Moabites, knew that the people of Israel were coming near to his land, he sent messengers, laden with presents, unto Balaam, the son of Beor, begging him to come and curse the Israelites, who were coming against him. But God had told Balaam he should not go, and Balaam was compelled to say no to the messengers. When they brought back this answer to Balak, he thought that he had not sent rich enough presents or noble enough men. So he, taking men of higher station and costlier presents, sent again to Balaam begging him to come and curse the Israelites. This time God told Balaam he might go, but could not say anything but what God put into his mouth.

When Balak knew that Balaam was coming he went out to meet him, and taking him up to a high place, where he could overlook the whole camp of Israel, again begged him to curse the Israelites. Balaam requested that seven altars be built there and seven oxen slain upon them. This was done. Then Balaam began to curse the people of Israel, but his curse turned into a blessing. Balak was very angry, but took him to a second high place, but again he blessed them. Also a third time did his intended curse come forth a blessing. Balak angrily cried: "Did I not bring you here to curse this people of Israel, and lo! you have blessed them these three times." Then answered Balaam: "How can I curse those whom God has not cursed?" And so it is, do your duty to God and to your fellow-beings and you can withstand the curses of all men.

The Israelites then fought against Balak, conquered him and took complete possession of his land.

They had now come up to the very border of the promised land, in sight of it, the Jordan River only between them and it, for, going around the land of Edom, they had come up east of Palestine, instead of south of it, as they would have done had they gone through Edom.

―――o―――

XLVII. DEATH OF MOSES.

Here the work of Moses was done. He was not to enter this holy land, and so he knew his end was near. He had been the faithful servant of God, had patiently and bravely borne with the fretful children of Israel during all their petty grievances and grumblings, had led them so gently under the guidance of the Almighty, during their forty years' wandering, and, after countless trials and troubles had brought them safely to the threshold of their new home, into which they had only to step. His life's mission was over, his duty fulfilled, his charge nobly carried out. He assembled the people together for the last time, read before them the law of God, recounted to them all His infinite and tender mercies, and begged them to remember all this, to be grateful to God, always to worship Him, and forsake the worship of senseless, lifeless, motionless idols of clay and stone and wood. He took Joshua out from among the people, and placing upon him the charge and leadership of the people, he urged and exhorted them to ever obey him.

Having performed this, he bade farewell to the people who were standing around, in tearful silence, taking a last look at their great leader who was to leave them so soon. When his last duty was done, Moses turned and went to the summit of Mt. Nebo, slowly disappearing from the sight of the sorrowing people to whom he never again appeared.

He died on Mt. Nebo, and no man knows his resting place. So there passed away the great, the good and kind Moses, the leader and lawgiver of our people, the servant and prophet of God.

www.ingramcontent.com/pod-product-compliance
Lightning Source LLC
Chambersburg PA
CBHW020900160426
43192CB00007B/1009